OTHER GIFTBOOKS IN THIS SERIES

baby boy!   *dad*   *mum*
happy day!   *smile*   *hope! dream!*
friend   *love*

Printed simultaneously in 2004 by Helen Exley Giftbooks
in Great Britain and Helen Exley Giftbooks LLC in the USA.

12 11 10 9 8 7 6 5 4 3 2 1

Illustrations © Joanna Kidney 2004
Copyright © Helen Exley 2004
Text copyright – see page 94
The moral right of the author has been asserted.

ISBN 1-86187-761-7

A copy of the CIP data is available from the British Library on request.
All rights reserved. No part of this publication may be reproduced
or transmitted in any form or by any means without permission.

Edited by Helen Exley
Pictures by Joanna Kidney

Printed in China

Helen Exley Giftbooks, 16 Chalk Hill, Watford, Herts WD19 4BG, UK.
Helen Exley Giftbooks LLC, 185 Main Street, Spencer MA 01562, USA.
www.helenexleygiftbooks.com

A HELEN EXLEY GIFTBOOK

baby girl!

PICTURES BY JOANNA KIDNEY

Babies are necessary to grown-ups.
A new baby is like the beginning
of all things
– wonder, hope,
a dream of possibilities.

EDA LESHAN (1922–2002)

I'LL NEVER FORGET THE FIRST TIME
I SAW YOU.
YOU WERE WET, STICKY, WRINKLY
AND SCREAMING YOUR HEAD OFF.
THE MOST PERFECT, BEAUTIFUL SIGHT
I HAD EVER SEEN.

STUART MACFARLANE, B.1953

Every baby born
into the world is a finer one
than the last.

CHARLES DICKENS (1812–1870),
FROM "NICHOLAS NICKLEBY"

The baby arrives
and the world is turned upside down.

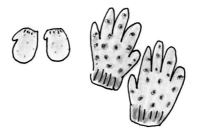

How utterly irrelevant are things
that yesterday seemed
vitally important.

MARION C. GARRETTY, B.1917

The whisper of a baby girl
can be heard further than
the roar of a lion.

ARAB PROVERB

Only when holding
your new baby gently
in your arms do you experience
the true meaning of love
– unconditional,
total,
complete surrender
to her every need.

STUART AND LINDA MACFARLANE

Babies are such

a nice way to start people.

DON HEROLD

When we hear
the baby laugh,
it is the loveliest thing
that can happen to us.

SIGMUND FREUD (1856–1939)

My number one priority is baby Jo....
A smile, a dimple, a kiss
– there is not a drink
that has ever been brewed that can hold
a candle to these delights.

ANTHONY BOOTH, FROM "THIS WEEK DAILY EXPRESS",
NOVEMBER 1994

Welcoming a newborn baby
is somehow absolute,
truer
and more binding than
any other experience
life has to offer.

MARILYN FRENCH, B.1929

I thought back to my past conviction
that only when I had a baby
would I *know* whatever it was I had to know.
Now I *did* know.
It is the only important thing
I have ever learned,
and so ridiculously simple: love exists.

LESLIE KENTON,
FROM "ALL I EVER WANTED WAS A BABY"

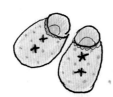

She held my attention
like a fiery constellation.
                    Her eyes bewitched me.
        Her first smile caused me and Jon
            to waltz around the room
    with the baby between us.
                We were besotted with her,
        the first parents in history.

ERICA JONG, B.1942, FROM "FEAR OF FIFTY"

A BABY. AN ASTONISHMENT.

A PERFECTION.

THE NEWEST THING IN THE WORLD.

SO SMALL.

SO PACKED WITH SECRETS.

PAM BROWN, B.1928

She was born, squawling
and berating the air, her face stripped
of its wisdom and serenity.
She seemed lost and confused,
helplessly dependent
upon physical surroundings
of which she had no knowledge.
Then someone placed her in my arms.
She looked up at me.
The crying stopped.

Her eyes melted through me,

forging a connection in me

with their soft heat.

I felt her love power stir in my heart.

SHIRLEY MACLAINE, B.1934

When I first laid eyes on Elizabeth
and she on me, it was recognition.
I knew her,
I knew that was what she looked like,
smelled like, sounded like.
It was amazing
because I could see in her eyes
that she knew me too...
I definitely felt a wave of love
flow back and forth.

PATRICIA BARTLETT

Loveliness beyond
completeness,
Sweetness distancing
all sweetness,
Beauty
all that beauty
may be –
That's May Bennett,
that's my baby.

WILLIAM COX BENNETT

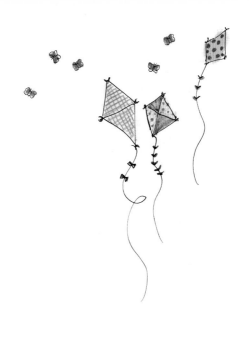

She holds out her hand to air,
Sea, sky, wind, sun,
movement, stillness.
And wants to hold them all.
My finger is her earth connection,
me, and earth.

JENNIFER ARMITAGE,
FROM "TO OUR DAUGHTER"

She is so beautiful,
so funny,
so eager, so resolute.
And she loves you
with all her heart.

PAM BROWN, B.1928

How can one
say no to a child?
How can one be
anything but a slave

to one's own flesh and blood?

HENRY MILLER (1891–1980)

I creep into her room
and stare down at her.
Smooth baby skin,
beautiful sleeping face
and soft, downy fair hair,
I'd rather look than pick her up,
my brand new daughter –
I'm still scared I'll harm her
with my awkwardness.

NICHOLE SWAIN

Babies... quickly realize
that expressions such as "Time to sleep"
and "Goodnight"
are but opportunities to be gently cradled
in a tender lap,
cheerfully listening to lullabies
for hour after hour after hour.

STUART AND LINDA MACFARLANE

Babies wake in the night and cry.
But as much sleep is lost
by first-time parents
in tiptoeing to the crib
to check that the child
is still breathing.

PAM BROWN, B.1928

The art of being a successful parent
is being able to sleep
in the ten-minute interludes
between putting food in one end
and it spluttering out of the other.

STUART AND LINDA MACFARLANE

You learn to love in a different way
– in the blurred world of night feeds,
colic, sniffles,
teething, tantrums, flung food
and sudden scares.

PAM BROWN, B.1928

The first lesson
a new father learns
is how to obey
his child's
every wish.

STUART AND LINDA MACFARLANE

MY WISHES FOR BABY

Small treasures.

Whorled shells and stripy stones,

toys carved or stitched

with love and care.

A pair of shiny shoes.

Music to dance to.

Daisies. A drowsiness of story telling.

A bear to hug.

A drifting into sleep.

PAM BROWN, B.1928

She looks around her and as she looks
She renews all she sees.
The leaves rustle excitedly,
The curtains dance by the window,
The shadow moves beside her as
She turns and she turns and she turns,
Ocean eyes,
Taking it all in.

SALLY EMERSON, FROM "BACK TO WORK"

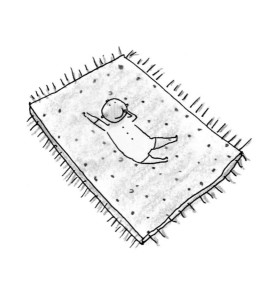

Watch a sixteen-stone dad
attempting to feed
a small stubborn baby
– and discover that determination
is not decided by weight.

PAM BROWN, B.1928

Daughters are a delight.
No one responds
with so complete a rapture to one's

offerings of farmyard imitations,
or small suprises.

PAMELA DUGDALE

You have at last
a legitimate excuse to splash,
play ducks

and wallow in baby foam bath.

PAM BROWN, B.1928

Her face lights up when you
– most ordinary you – come into sight.
Your songs delight her.
You are the one
who can soothe her into sleep,
drive off her terrors,
lever her from tears to laughter.

PAM BROWN, B.1928

A daughter is a new beginning.
A daughter is your excuse
for making a dolls' house.
A daughter is the person you think
you will stop worrying about
when she hits twenty-one.
But will still worry you at forty-five.

PAM BROWN, B.1928

Wrapped around her little finger?!
Not at all!!
I *wanted*
to buy her
all those teddies,
dolls,
books....

STUART MACFARLANE, B.1953

Dad has long and earnest conversations
with his baby daughter.
He tells her she is noisy, undisciplined
and manipulative
– and she will be sent back
if she doesn't pull herself together.
And the baby smiles complacently.
She has him *exactly*
where she wants him.

PAM BROWN, B.1928

＊ ＊ ＊ ＊ ＊ ＊ ＊ ＊ ＊

I love my little girl an extraordinary amount;
Since her birth I have been
        so wholly preoccupied
with the minutiae of her progress –
   from the growth of the microscopic hairs
     on her bald head
        to the lengthening of her attention span
– that I have been effectively lost
        to the larger world.

HARRY STEIN, FROM "ESQUIRE"

I have made a baby board for you
my daughter
Of the sun's rays I have made the back
Of black clouds I have made the blanket
Of rainbow I have made the bow
Of sunbeams I have made the side loops
Of dawn have
I made the bed covering.

NAVAJO CHANT

No one told you
that the change was irreversible.
That you would feel
in your own heart every pain,
every loss,
every disappointment,
every rebuff,
every cruelty that she experiences
— life long.

ROSANNE AMBROSE-BROWN, B.1943

For daughters the world is full of marvels
they will share with you –
pointing to blossoming trees
and rainbow puddles.

PAMELA DUGDALE

...my darling girl

Sleeps and smiles and laughs,

her face
> So full of curiosity and magic
That I know the world was
> Made in her honour.

SALLY EMERSON, FROM "BACK TO WORK"

You dream – I see the images flicker
across your face – and yet –
what can a baby dream?
I kiss away your fears –
and hold you, safe from every harm.
Sleep
– and grow in wonder
and contentment.

PETER GRAY, B.1928

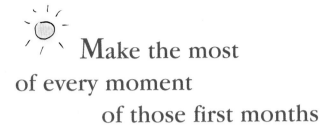

Make the most
of every moment
of those first months

– they will never come again.

PAM BROWN, B.1928

...You will never be free again.
You live two lives now,
                    hers and your own.
        There will be nights without sleep.
And happiness beyond
            anything you ever thought possible.
            Surprises. Amazement.
        For she is your diamond daughter.

ROSANNE AMBROSE-BROWN, B.1943

Daughters will do
wonderful things,
astonishing things,

better than you ever dreamed.

MARION C. GARRETTY, B.1917

We find delight in the beauty
      and happiness of children
that makes the heart
      too big for the body.

RALPH WALDO EMERSON (1803–1882)

Enchanting is that baby-laugh,
all dimples and glitter –
      so strangely warm and innocent.

MARGARET F. OSSOLI (1810–1850)

All babies bring Spring
back to the world.

PAM BROWN, B.1928

Helen Exley runs her own publishing company which sells giftbooks in more than seventy countries. She had always wanted to do a little book on smiles, and had been collecting the quotations for many years, but always felt that the available illustrations just weren't quite right. Then Helen fell in love with Joanna Kidney's happy, bright pictures and knew immediately they had the feel she was looking for. She asked Joanna to work on *smile*, and then to go on to contribute the art for four more books: *friend*, *happy day!*, *love* and *hope! dream!* We are now publishing five more books in this series, *dad*, *mum*, *baby boy!*, *baby girl!* and *wedding*.

Joanna Kidney lives in County Wicklow in Ireland. She juggles her time between working on various illustration projects and producing her own art for shows and exhibitions. Her whole range of greeting cards, *Joanna's Pearlies* – some of which appear in this book – won the prestigious 2001 Henries oscar for 'best fun or graphic range'.

Text Copyright: The publishers are grateful for permission to reproduce copyright material. Whilst every reasonable effort has been made to trace copyright holders, the publishers would be pleased to hear from any not here acknowledged.
PAM BROWN, ROSANNE AMBROSE-BROWN, PAMELA DUGDALE, MARION
C. GARRETTY, PETER GRAY, STUART AND LINDA MACFARLANE © HELEN EXLEY 2004.